BSV
UNLEASHING THE FUTURE BLOCKCHAIN

LEGAL DISCLAIMER

Chapter 1

Introduction to Bitcoin SV

Bitcoin SV (BSV) emerged as a significant player in the world of cryptocurrencies, building upon the original vision outlined by Satoshi Nakamoto in the Bitcoin whitepaper. In this chapter, we will explore the foundations of Bitcoin SV, its history, and its key features.

1.1 The Origins of Bitcoin and Forks

To understand Bitcoin SV, we must first revisit the origins of Bitcoin itself. In 2008, an anonymous individual or group named Satoshi Nakamoto introduced Bitcoin as a peer-to-peer electronic cash system. Bitcoin aimed to enable secure, decentralized transactions without the need for intermediaries like banks.

Over the years, the Bitcoin community experienced disagreements about the direction of the protocol, leading to several forks or splits. Two notable forks were Bitcoin Cash (BCH) and Bitcoin SV (BSV). Bitcoin Cash emerged in 2017, primarily focusing on increasing block sizes to address scalability concerns. However, differences in the community's vision eventually led to the creation of Bitcoin SV.

1.2 The Vision of Bitcoin SV

Bitcoin SV's primary objective is to restore the original Bitcoin protocol and stay true to Satoshi Nakamoto's vision. The acronym "SV" stands for "Satoshi Vision," emphasizing its commitment to preserving the foundational principles of Bitcoin.

Key aspects of Bitcoin SV's vision include:

1.2.1 Scalability: Bitcoin SV recognizes the importance of scaling the network to handle a high volume of transactions efficiently. It aims to achieve this by increasing the block size and enabling faster transaction processing.

1.2.2 Stability: Stability and reliability are crucial for any financial system. Bitcoin SV aims to provide a stable platform for transactions and applications, ensuring a predictable and robust ecosystem for users and developers.

1.2.3 Security: Bitcoin SV places a strong emphasis on security. By employing advanced cryptographic techniques and decentralized consensus mechanisms, it aims to protect the network from potential attacks and maintain the integrity of transactions.

1.2.4 Low Transaction Fees: Bitcoin SV aims to keep transaction fees low, making it cost-effective for users to conduct everyday transactions on the network. This affordability is essential for encouraging widespread adoption and usability.

1.3 Notable Features of Bitcoin SV

Bitcoin SV brings several notable features to the table,

differentiating itself from other cryptocurrencies. Some key features include:

1.3.1 Larger Block Sizes: Bitcoin SV supports significantly larger block sizes compared to Bitcoin and other cryptocurrencies. This capability allows for more transactions to be included in each block, increasing throughput and scalability.

1.3.2 Enhanced Transaction Processing: With larger blocks, Bitcoin SV can process a higher number of transactions per second, aiming to handle a higher volume of on-chain transactions efficiently.

1.3.3 Scripting and Smart Contracts: Bitcoin SV extends the capabilities of the original Bitcoin protocol by incorporating scripting functionality. This allows for the creation of more complex smart contracts and the development of decentralized applications (DApps) on the BSV blockchain.

1.3.4 Data Storage: Bitcoin SV's Metanet protocol enables the storage and management of large amounts of data on the blockchain. This feature opens up possibilities for innovative applications, such as verifiable document storage, intellectual property management, and content monetization.

Bitcoin SV represents an evolution of the Bitcoin protocol, seeking to fulfill the original vision of Satoshi Nakamoto. With its focus on scalability, stability, security, and low transaction fees, Bitcoin SV aims to provide a robust and user-friendly platform for transactions and decentralized applications. In the subsequent chapters, we will explore various aspects of Bitcoin SV in greater detail, uncovering its potential use cases, technical intricacies, and its impact on the broader financial landscape.

Chapter 2

Understanding Blockchain Technology

In this chapter, we will delve into

the fundamental concepts of blockchain technology to gain a better understanding of how Bitcoin SV operates. We will explore the key components that make up a blockchain, the underlying principles behind its functionality, and its role in enabling secure and decentralized transactions.

2.1 What is a Blockchain?

At its core, a blockchain is a decentralized and distributed digital ledger that records transactions across multiple computers or nodes. Each transaction is grouped into a block and added to a chain of previous blocks, forming a chronological sequence of transactions.

The blockchain's decentralized nature means that no single entity or authority has control over the entire network. Instead, it relies on a consensus mechanism, typically achieved through a consensus algorithm like Proof of Work (PoW) or Proof of Stake (PoS), to validate and agree upon the contents of the blockchain.

2.2 Key Components of a Blockchain

To understand how a blockchain operates, it is essential to grasp its key components:

2.2.1 Blocks: Blocks are the building blocks of a blockchain. They contain a set of transactions, a timestamp, and a unique identifier called a hash. Each block is linked to the previous block through its hash, creating an unbroken chain of blocks.

2.2.2 Transactions: Transactions represent the transfer of value or information within the blockchain network. Each transaction typically includes information such as the sender, recipient, amount, and additional data related to the transaction.

2.2.3 Hashing: Hashing is a cryptographic process that converts an input (such as a block or transaction) into a fixed-length alphanumeric string. This hash serves as a unique identifier for the data and ensures its integrity. Even a slight change in the input data will produce a drastically different hash value.

2.2.4 Consensus Mechanism: Consensus mechanisms enable agreement among network participants on the validity and order of transactions. Common consensus algorithms include Proof of Work (PoW), where participants compete to solve complex mathematical problems to add blocks, and Proof of Stake (PoS), where validators are chosen based on the number of coins they hold.

2.3 Decentralization and Security

Decentralization is a core principle of blockchain technology. By distributing the ledger across multiple nodes, a blockchain eliminates the need for a central authority and provides greater resilience against single points of failure and manipulation.

The security of a blockchain is achieved through cryptographic techniques. Transactions are secured using public-key cryptography, where each participant possesses a pair of cryptographic keys: a private key for signing transactions and a public key for verification.

Additionally, the consensus mechanism ensures that the majority of participants agree on the state of the blockchain. This agreement makes it extremely difficult for malicious actors to tamper with transaction history or forge fraudulent transactions.

2.4 The Role of Bitcoin SV in Blockchain Technology

Bitcoin SV builds upon the principles of blockchain

technology, utilizing its core features to enable secure and transparent transactions. It embraces the decentralized nature of blockchain and leverages the consensus mechanism to validate and record transactions on the BSV network.

The larger block sizes of Bitcoin SV facilitate a higher transaction throughput, allowing for more transactions to be processed within a given time frame. This scalability is crucial for accommodating a growing user base and fostering widespread adoption.

Furthermore, Bitcoin SV's scripting capabilities enable the development of smart contracts and decentralized applications (DApps) on the BSV blockchain. These features empower developers to build innovative solutions that can leverage the transparency and security of the blockchain.

Blockchain technology forms the foundation of Bitcoin SV's functionality. By embracing the decentralized, secure, and transparent nature of blockchain, Bitcoin SV aims to provide a robust and efficient platform for peer-to-peer transactions. Understanding the core components and principles of blockchain technology lays the groundwork for exploring the specific advancements and unique features of Bitcoin SV, which we will delve into in subsequent chapters.

Chapter 3

The Scaling Debate and Bitcoin SV

One of the most significant challenges faced by blockchain networks, including Bitcoin, is scalability. In this chapter, we will explore the scaling debate that emerged within the Bitcoin community and how Bitcoin SV addresses this challenge through its approach to scaling.

3.1 The Need for Scalability

Scalability refers to the ability of a blockchain network to handle a large number of transactions quickly and efficiently. As Bitcoin gained popularity, its limited block size and block time posed scalability issues. With a small block size and a fixed block time of approximately 10 minutes, Bitcoin's transaction throughput was constrained.

As the number of users and transactions increased, the network became congested, leading to higher transaction fees and longer confirmation times. This scalability challenge prompted a heated debate within the Bitcoin community on how to address the issue.

3.2 The Bitcoin Scaling Debate

The Bitcoin scaling debate revolved around two primary proposals:

3.2.1 Segregated Witness (SegWit):

SegWit aimed to increase the transaction capacity of Bitcoin by separating the transaction signature (witness data) from the transaction data, effectively reducing the amount of data required to be stored in each block.

3.2.2 Bigger Blocks: An alternative proposal suggested increasing the block size limit to accommodate more transactions per block. Advocates argued that larger blocks would allow for a higher transaction throughput, reducing congestion and transaction fees.

3.3 Bitcoin Cash and the Emergence of Bitcoin SV

The Bitcoin scaling debate led to a significant fork in the blockchain, resulting in the creation of Bitcoin Cash (BCH) in August 2017. Bitcoin Cash increased the block size from 1MB to 8MB, enabling more transactions to be included in each block.

However, disagreements within the Bitcoin Cash community regarding the future direction of the protocol led to another fork. On November 15, 2018, Bitcoin SV (BSV) emerged as a separate entity, led by proponents seeking to restore the original Bitcoin protocol and its vision.

3.4 Bitcoin SV's Approach to Scaling

Bitcoin SV's approach to scaling revolves around the concept of larger block sizes. By increasing the block size limit, Bitcoin SV aims to achieve higher transaction throughput and improved scalability. Initially set at 128MB, the block size limit on the BSV network has been further increased to support even larger blocks.

The larger block sizes enable more transactions to be processed within each block, reducing congestion and transaction fees. Bitcoin SV proponents argue that this approach aligns with Satoshi Nakamoto's original vision of Bitcoin as a peer-to-peer electronic cash system capable of handling a significant number of transactions.

3.5 Benefits and Criticisms of Bitcoin SV's Scaling Approach

Bitcoin SV's focus on larger block sizes has both benefits and criticisms:

3.5.1 Benefits:

Increased Transaction Throughput: Larger blocks allow

for a higher volume of transactions to be processed within a given time frame, improving the overall transaction throughput of the network.

Lower Transaction Fees: With more space available in each block, Bitcoin SV aims to keep transaction fees lower compared to other blockchain networks, making it cost-effective for everyday transactions.

3.5.2 Criticisms:

Centralization Concerns: Critics argue that larger block sizes may lead to increased centralization, as the computational and storage requirements for processing and storing larger blocks could pose challenges for individual participants.

Network Bandwidth and Storage Requirements: Processing and validating larger blocks require significant network bandwidth and storage capabilities, which could be a barrier for full node operators, potentially impacting the network's decentralization.

The scalability challenge has been a key point of contention within the Bitcoin community. Bitcoin SV emerged as a distinct entity aiming to address this challenge by advocating for larger block sizes and increasing transaction throughput. By embracing larger blocks, Bitcoin SV aims to offer a scalable and efficient platform for peer-to-peer transactions. However, the approach has sparked debates regarding centralization concerns and the requirements for network participants. In the following chapters, we will further explore the technical advancements and use cases of Bitcoin SV, shedding light on its potential and impact in the blockchain ecosystem.

Chapter 4

The Genesis Upgrade

In the development of Bitcoin SV, a significant milestone known as the Genesis upgrade took place. In this chapter, we will explore the Genesis upgrade, its purpose, and the changes it brought to the Bitcoin SV network.

4.1 Understanding the Genesis Upgrade

The Genesis upgrade refers to a significant hard fork that occurred on the Bitcoin SV (BSV) network on February 4, 2020. This upgrade marked a pivotal moment in the evolution of Bitcoin SV and aimed to restore the original Bitcoin protocol as outlined by Satoshi Nakamoto.

The Genesis upgrade involved the implementation of several important changes to the Bitcoin

SV network, including the following:

4.2 Return to the Original Bitcoin Protocol

The Genesis upgrade sought to reset the Bitcoin SV blockchain to its original state, removing unnecessary opcodes and restoring various technical aspects of the Bitcoin protocol. The intention was to align Bitcoin SV more closely with Satoshi

Nakamoto's original vision for Bitcoin.

4.3 Op_Return Data Size Increase

One significant change introduced in the Genesis upgrade was the increase in the maximum size of OP_RETURN data within a transaction. OP_RETURN is an opcode used to embed data into a Bitcoin transaction, allowing for various applications beyond simple value transfer. The upgrade expanded the size limit, enabling greater flexibility and potential use cases for storing data on the blockchain.

4.4 Restriction on Uncommon Script Operations

To enhance network security and ensure compliance with standard Bitcoin operations, the Genesis upgrade imposed restrictions on uncommon script operations. This change aimed to streamline and simplify the Bitcoin SV network by removing unnecessary or unutilized script operations, making it more efficient and secure.

4.5 Transaction Ordering Rules

The Genesis upgrade also introduced changes to the transaction ordering rules. It modified how transactions are prioritized and ordered within a block, improving the fairness and reliability of transaction processing.

4.6 The Purpose of the Genesis Upgrade

The Genesis upgrade had several key purposes:

4.6.1 Restoration of the Original Protocol: The upgrade aimed to bring Bitcoin SV back to the original Bitcoin protocol envisioned by Satoshi Nakamoto.

By removing unnecessary elements and aligning with the original design, Bitcoin SV intended to remain true to the core principles and goals of Bitcoin.

4.6.2 Enhanced Stability and Security: The upgrade sought to enhance the stability and security of the Bitcoin SV network by removing unused or potentially vulnerable features and refining the transaction ordering rules.

4.6.3 Long-term Vision and Development: The Genesis upgrade represented a commitment to the long-term vision and development of Bitcoin SV as a robust and scalable blockchain platform. It set the stage for further advancements and innovations within the Bitcoin SV ecosystem.

The Genesis upgrade was a critical event in the evolution of Bitcoin

SV. It aimed to restore the original Bitcoin protocol and bring the network closer to Satoshi Nakamoto's vision. Through this upgrade, Bitcoin SV underwent significant changes, including the removal of unnecessary opcodes, the expansion of OP_RETURN data size, and the refinement of transaction ordering rules. The Genesis upgrade reaffirmed Bitcoin SV's commitment to its long-term goals and paved the way for future developments and innovations within the network.

Chapter 5

Smart Contracts and Tokenization on Bitcoin SV

Bitcoin SV (BSV) extends the functionality of the blockchain beyond simple transactions, enabling the development of smart contracts and tokenization. In this chapter, we will explore the concepts of smart contracts and tokenization and how Bitcoin SV facilitates their implementation.

5.1 Understanding Smart Contracts

Smart contracts are self-executing agreements with predefined conditions encoded directly into the blockchain. These contracts automatically execute and enforce the terms of an agreement without the need for intermediaries.

Bitcoin SV provides a platform for developing and deploying smart contracts. Smart contracts on BSV can facilitate various types of transactions, including multi-signature transactions, time-locked transactions, and conditional payments. This programmability enables the creation of complex financial arrangements and automated processes directly on the blockchain.

5.2 Tokenization on Bitcoin SV

Tokenization refers to the process of representing real-world assets or digital goods as tokens on a blockchain. Tokens can represent a wide range of assets, such as real estate, stocks, commodities, or even unique digital items like in-game assets.

Bitcoin SV supports tokenization, allowing individuals and businesses to create and manage their own tokens on the BSV blockchain. These tokens can have unique properties, including ownership rights, transferability, and programmable functionalities.

5.3 Advantages of Smart Contracts and Tokenization on Bitcoin SV

Implementing smart contracts and tokenization on Bitcoin SV brings several advantages:

5.3.1 Increased Efficiency and Automation: Smart contracts

automate the execution of agreements, eliminating the need for manual intervention. This improves efficiency, reduces costs, and minimizes the potential for human error.

5.3.2 Improved Transparency and Security: Smart contracts on Bitcoin SV provide transparent and auditable transactions. The blockchain's immutability ensures that contract terms and transaction history cannot be altered, enhancing security and trust.

5.3.3 Programmable Money: Smart contracts allow for programmable money, enabling the development of sophisticated financial applications and decentralized autonomous organizations (DAOs). These applications can operate autonomously based on predefined rules and conditions.

5.3.4 Fractional Ownership and Liquidity: Tokenization enables fractional ownership, making it easier to divide assets into smaller units. This opens up opportunities for broader participation in investments and increases liquidity for traditionally illiquid assets.

5.3.5 Simplified Compliance and Regulation: Smart contracts can enforce compliance with regulatory requirements by embedding the necessary rules and conditions directly into the contract code. This helps streamline compliance processes and reduces the risk of non-compliance.

5.4 Real-World Applications of Smart Contracts and Tokenization on Bitcoin SV

The combination of smart contracts and tokenization on Bitcoin SV unlocks a wide range of potential applications across various industries:

5.4.1 Supply Chain Management: Smart contracts and tokenization can streamline supply chain processes, improving transparency, traceability, and accountability in the movement of goods and assets.

5.4.2 Intellectual Property Rights: Tokenization allows for the fractional ownership of intellectual property rights, enabling creators to monetize their work and enforce copyright protection.

5.4.3 Financial Services: Smart contracts can automate traditional financial services, such as lending, insurance, and asset management, reducing costs and improving efficiency.

5.4.4 Gaming and Digital Collectibles: Tokenization

facilitates the creation of in-game assets, digital collectibles, and virtual economies, allowing for verifiable ownership and secure peer-to-peer trading.

5.4.5 Real Estate: Tokenization can make real estate investments more accessible by dividing properties into fractional tokens, enabling broader participation and increasing liquidity in the real estate market.

Bitcoin SV's support for smart contracts and tokenization extends the capabilities of the blockchain beyond simple transactions. By enabling programmable agreements and representing real-world assets as tokens, Bitcoin SV opens up new possibilities for automation, efficiency, and innovative applications. The combination of smart contracts and tokenization has the potential to transform various industries, offering increased transparency, improved security, and expanded financial opportunities. In the subsequent chapters, we will explore further technical details and use cases to understand the broader impact of smart contracts and tokenization on Bitcoin SV.

Chapter 6

Metanet and Data Storage on Bitcoin SV

Bitcoin SV (BSV) introduces the concept of Metanet, a groundbreaking framework that combines blockchain and the internet. In this chapter, we will explore Metanet and its implications for data storage, management, and monetization on the BSV blockchain.

6.1 Understanding Metanet

Metanet refers to an integrated system that leverages the Bitcoin SV blockchain to create a new paradigm for data storage and management. It envisions a seamless integration of the blockchain and the internet, enabling a more efficient, transparent, and monetizable data ecosystem.

Metanet views the internet as an application layer built on top of the Bitcoin SV blockchain, with data stored directly on the blockchain and indexed for easy retrieval and monetization. It aims to enable a decentralized internet where users have greater control over their data and can directly monetize their digital assets.

6.2 Data Storage and Retrieval on the Metanet

In the Metanet framework, data is stored directly on the Bitcoin SV blockchain, utilizing the secure and immutable nature of the blockchain. This approach ensures the integrity and permanence of the data, reducing the reliance on centralized servers or intermediaries.

Each piece of data on the Metanet is assigned a unique identifier known as a Metanet ID. This ID acts as a reference to the data, making it easily discoverable and retrievable by users. The Metanet ID can also contain metadata that provides additional information about the data, enabling efficient search and categorization.

6.3 Benefits of Metanet Data Storage

The integration of data storage with the Bitcoin SV blockchain through Metanet brings several benefits:

6.3.1 Immutable and Verifiable Data: Storing data on the blockchain ensures its immutability and verifiability. Once recorded on the blockchain, the data cannot be altered or tampered with, providing a reliable and trustworthy source of information.

6.3.2 Enhanced Security and Privacy: The decentralized nature of the blockchain combined with cryptographic techniques ensures the security and privacy of data stored on the Metanet. Users have control over their data and can choose the level of visibility or privacy they desire.

6.3.3 Monetization Opportunities: Metanet opens up new avenues for data monetization. By directly storing data on the blockchain, creators can retain ownership and control over their digital assets, allowing for direct monetization through micropayments, licensing, or other revenue models.

6.3.4 Efficient Data Management: Metanet provides a more efficient system for managing and organizing data. The use of Metanet IDs and metadata enables quick and targeted retrieval of specific data, making it easier to navigate and analyze large volumes of information.

6.4 Applications of Metanet

Metanet has the potential to transform various industries and applications:

6.4.1 Content Publishing: Metanet enables content creators to publish their work directly on the blockchain, ensuring copyright protection and enabling direct monetization through micropayments or other revenue models.

6.4.2 Intellectual Property Rights: The immutability and transparency of the blockchain make it an ideal platform for managing and enforcing intellectual property rights. Creators can store evidence of their work on the blockchain, establishing a verifiable timestamp and ownership.

6.4.3 Data Marketplace: Metanet can facilitate the creation of decentralized data marketplaces, where individuals and businesses can trade and exchange data directly, bypassing intermediaries and ensuring fair compensation for data providers.

6.4.4 Identity Management: Metanet can be used for decentralized identity management, where users have control over their personal data and can selectively share it with trusted entities, enhancing privacy and security.

6.5   Challenges   and   Future Developments

While Metanet presents exciting opportunities, there are challenges to overcome. These include scalability considerations, ensuring data privacy and security, and addressing regulatory and legal frameworks for data storage and monetization.

The development of Metanet is an ongoing process, with continuous innovation and improvements. As the Bitcoin SV ecosystem evolves, we can expect further advancements, tools, and applications to enhance the Metanet framework and expand its reach into different industries.

Metanet represents a visionary concept that combines blockchain and the internet, offering a new paradigm for data storage, management, and monetization. By leveraging the Bitcoin SV blockchain, Metanet provides a secure, efficient, and transparent platform for storing and retrieving data, empowering individuals and businesses to take control of their digital assets. The potential applications of Metanet are vast, from content publishing and intellectual property management to data marketplaces and decentralized identity systems. As the development of Metanet progresses, it promises to reshape the way we store, manage, and monetize data in the digital age.

Chapter 7

Regulatory and Legal Considerations for Bitcoin SV

As cryptocurrencies gain prominence, regulatory and legal considerations become increasingly important. In this chapter, we will delve into the regulatory landscape surrounding Bitcoin SV (BSV) and the challenges and opportunities it presents.

7.1 Regulatory Frameworks and Bitcoin SV

Bitcoin SV operates within existing regulatory frameworks, subject to laws and regulations governing financial transactions, securities, anti-money laundering (AML), and know-your-customer (KYC) requirements. The specific regulatory landscape for Bitcoin SV varies from country to country and is continuously evolving.

7.2 Challenges in Regulatory Compliance

Complying with existing regulations poses challenges for the Bitcoin SV ecosystem:

7.2.1 AML and KYC Requirements: Bitcoin SV entities, such as exchanges and financial service providers, often face the challenge of implementing robust AML and KYC measures to ensure compliance with regulations.

These measures help prevent illicit activities, such as money laundering and terrorist financing.

7.2.2 Jurisdictional Variances: The lack of harmonized global regulations for cryptocurrencies can lead to inconsistencies and jurisdictional complexities. Entities operating across multiple jurisdictions need to navigate varying regulatory requirements and adapt their practices accordingly.

7.2.3 Regulatory Uncertainty: The evolving nature of cryptocurrency regulation can create uncertainty for businesses and individuals operating within the Bitcoin SV ecosystem. Clarity and consistency in regulatory guidelines are crucial for fostering innovation and attracting investment.

7.3 Regulatory Opportunities and Advancements

While regulatory challenges exist, there are also opportunities and advancements within the regulatory landscape:

7.3.1 Clarity and Consumer Protection: Clear and well-defined regulations can provide

Chapter 8

Security and Privacy on Bitcoin SV

Security and privacy are critical aspects of any blockchain system. In this chapter, we will explore the security measures implemented in Bitcoin SV (BSV) to protect user funds and ensure the integrity of the network. We will also delve into the balance between privacy and transparency in BSV transactions.

8.1 Security Measures in Bitcoin SV

Bitcoin SV employs several security measures to safeguard the network and user funds:

8.1.1 Cryptographic Security:

Bitcoin SV utilizes robust cryptographic algorithms to secure transactions and ensure the integrity of data stored on the blockchain. Public-key cryptography protects users' private keys, enabling secure ownership and control of funds.

8.1.2 Decentralized Consensus: BSV's decentralized consensus mechanism, primarily based on Proof of Work (PoW), ensures that transactions and blocks are validated by a distributed network of nodes. This decentralization makes it difficult for malicious actors to manipulate the blockchain.

8.1.3 Immutable Transaction History: Once a transaction is confirmed and added to a block, it becomes part of the immutable transaction history on the BSV blockchain. This permanence ensures that transactions cannot be altered or tampered with, establishing a trustworthy and transparent record.

8.1.4 Secure Wallets and Storage: Users can employ secure wallet solutions to store their BSV securely. Hardware wallets, software wallets with strong encryption, and cold storage options provide added layers of protection against unauthorized access and theft.

8.2 Privacy and Transparency in BSV Transactions

Bitcoin SV balances the need for privacy with the desire for transparency:

8.2.1 Pseudonymous Nature: Bitcoin SV transactions are pseudonymous, as they are linked to cryptographic addresses rather than real-world identities. This pseudonymity protects user privacy by allowing transactions to be conducted without revealing personal information.

8.2.2 Transaction Transparency: While the identity of users is not directly associated with transactions, all Bitcoin SV transactions are transparent and traceable on the public blockchain. Transaction details, including sender and receiver addresses and transaction amounts, are visible to all network participants.

8.2.3 Privacy Enhancement Techniques: Additional privacy-enhancing techniques can be employed on top of the BSV network to increase transaction privacy. These techniques include coin mixing and privacy-focused wallet implementations that aim to obfuscate transaction trails.

8.3 Balancing Security and Privacy Considerations

Striking a balance between security and privacy is crucial in the design of a blockchain system like Bitcoin SV:

8.3.1 User Control and Responsibility: Bitcoin SV

empowers users to take control of their own security and privacy. Users must be vigilant in safeguarding their private keys, using secure wallets, and following best practices to protect their funds and personal information.

8.3.2 Regulatory Compliance: Security and privacy considerations must also align with regulatory requirements. Complying with AML and KYC regulations may involve certain compromises in terms of privacy, as businesses and individuals need to verify the identities of users to prevent illicit activities.

8.3.3 Innovations in Privacy Solutions: Ongoing research and development efforts focus on improving privacy solutions on the BSV network. Innovations such as Zero-Knowledge Proofs and advanced encryption techniques may offer enhanced privacy features while maintaining the integrity of the network.

Security and privacy are paramount in the Bitcoin SV ecosystem. Through cryptographic security, decentralized consensus, and immutable transaction history, Bitcoin SV ensures the integrity and trustworthiness of transactions. The pseudonymous nature of transactions provides privacy, while transparency and traceability on the public blockchain foster accountability. Striking a balance between security and privacy considerations is an ongoing challenge that requires user education, regulatory compliance, and continuous innovation in privacy solutions. Bitcoin SV aims to provide a secure and privacy-conscious platform for users, fostering trust and enabling the seamless transfer of value on the blockchain.

Chapter 9

Real-World Use Cases of Bitcoin SV

Bitcoin SV (BSV) holds promise for a wide range of real-world applications beyond simple transactions. In this chapter, we will explore some notable use cases that leverage the unique features and capabilities of Bitcoin SV, revolutionizing various industries and sectors.

9.1 Supply Chain Management

Supply chain management involves tracking and managing the flow of goods and services from their origin to the end consumer. Bitcoin SV offers transparency, traceability, and immutability, making it ideal for supply chain applications. By storing relevant information on the blockchain, such as product origins, certifications, and transportation details, stakeholders can ensure authenticity, reduce fraud, and enhance trust within the supply chain ecosystem.

9.2 Healthcare Records

Bitcoin SV can transform the management of healthcare records by providing a secure and transparent platform for storing and sharing sensitive patient information. By utilizing smart contracts and encryption techniques, patient data can be securely stored on the blockchain, ensuring privacy, interoperability, and easy access for authorized healthcare providers. This enables more efficient healthcare processes, reduces data breaches, and improves patient outcomes.

9.3 Intellectual Property Management

The immutable and timestamped nature of the Bitcoin SV

blockchain makes it an ideal platform for managing intellectual property (IP) rights. Creators can securely timestamp their work on the blockchain, providing proof of existence and establishing ownership. This can simplify the process of copyright registration and help protect against plagiarism and IP infringement. Tokenization on Bitcoin SV also enables the fractional ownership of IP rights, allowing creators to monetize their creations through licensing and royalty agreements.

9.4   Content Publishing and Micropayments

Bitcoin SV facilitates a new era of content publishing and monetization. Content creators can publish their work directly on the blockchain, ensuring copyright protection and establishing a direct relationship with consumers. Micropayments become viable through Bitcoin SV's low transaction fees, allowing users to pay small amounts for accessing premium content. This empowers creators by enabling direct monetization without relying on intermediaries, such as advertising platforms or subscription services.

9.5 Gaming and Digital Collectibles

Bitcoin SV has the potential to revolutionize the gaming industry by providing a decentralized and transparent platform for in-game assets and digital collectibles. Through tokenization, unique and verifiable digital items can be created, bought, sold, and traded on the blockchain. This fosters ownership, scarcity, and interoperability of virtual assets across different games, creating new opportunities for gamers and developers in the rapidly growing virtual economy.

9.6 Financial Services and Remittances

Bitcoin SV's programmable money and low transaction fees make it suitable for various financial services. It enables efficient remittance solutions, allowing cross-border transactions to be conducted quickly and cost-effectively. Additionally, the programmability of smart contracts on Bitcoin SV enables the development of decentralized finance (DeFi) applications, such as lending platforms, decentralized exchanges, and tokenized asset trading.

Bitcoin SV's unique features, including its scalability, smart contracts, and tokenization capabilities, open up a wide range of real-world use cases. From supply chain management and healthcare records to intellectual property management and content publishing, Bitcoin SV offers innovative solutions that enhance transparency, security, and efficiency across industries. As the ecosystem continues to evolve, we can expect further exploration and development of new applications and business models that harness the power of Bitcoin SV, shaping the future of decentralized systems and digital interactions.

Chapter 10

The Future of Bitcoin SV

Bitcoin SV (BSV) has made significant strides since its inception, but what does the future hold for this blockchain platform? In this chapter, we will explore the potential developments, challenges, and opportunities that lie ahead for Bitcoin SV.

10.1 Scalability and Adoption

Scalability remains a key focus for Bitcoin SV. As the network continues to grow, further advancements in block size and transaction throughput will be necessary to accommodate increased adoption. Ongoing research and development efforts aim to optimize scalability while maintaining the decentralization and security of the network.

Widespread adoption is crucial for the success of any blockchain platform, and Bitcoin SV is no exception. To achieve mainstream adoption, efforts will be made to simplify user experiences, enhance user interfaces, and create user-friendly applications that leverage the unique capabilities of the Bitcoin SV blockchain. Increasing merchant acceptance and integration of BSV as a payment option will also contribute to its wider adoption.

10.2 Regulation and Compliance

The regulatory landscape for cryptocurrencies continues to evolve, and Bitcoin SV will need to navigate these changing regulations. Striking a balance between compliance and the principles of decentralization and privacy will be a critical challenge. Collaboration with regulatory authorities and adherence to AML and KYC requirements will play a vital role in establishing trust and ensuring a compliant ecosystem.

Clarity and consistency in regulatory frameworks will be essential for fostering innovation and attracting institutional investment. Collaborative efforts between industry stakeholders, regulators, and policymakers can help shape regulatory guidelines that support responsible growth and development within the Bitcoin SV ecosystem.

10.3 Interoperability and Integration

Interoperability with other blockchain platforms and traditional systems will be an important aspect of Bitcoin SV's future development. Collaborations and partnerships with other projects and networks can unlock new opportunities and create synergies across different ecosystems. Standardization efforts and interoperability protocols will facilitate seamless integration, enabling cross-platform compatibility and data exchange.

Integration with existing systems and industries, such as supply chain management, healthcare, and finance, will be a key focus. Bridging the gap between blockchain technology and real-world applications will require ongoing collaboration and innovation to address specific industry needs and challenges.

10.4   Continued   Technical Advancements

Bitcoin SV will continue to evolve technologically, with ongoing research and development efforts focused on improving the platform's capabilities. Innovations in areas such as privacy solutions, scalability techniques, smart contract functionality, and tokenization will enhance the overall user experience and open up new possibilities for applications and use cases.

The BSV developer community will play a crucial role in driving these technical advancements. Continued support and investment in developer tools, resources, and education will foster a vibrant ecosystem of developers building innovative solutions on the Bitcoin SV blockchain.

The future of Bitcoin SV holds great promise. With a focus on scalability, adoption, regulation, interoperability, and technical advancements, Bitcoin SV aims to position itself as a leading blockchain platform for real-world applications. Overcoming challenges and seizing opportunities will require collaboration, education, and ongoing innovation. As Bitcoin SV continues to evolve, it has the potential to transform industries, drive economic growth, and empower individuals worldwide.

Chapter 11

The Community and Ecosystem of Bitcoin SV

Bitcoin SV (BSV) is more than just a blockchain platform—it is supported by a vibrant community and an expanding ecosystem. In this chapter, we will explore the community that surrounds Bitcoin SV, its values, achievements, and the diverse range of projects and initiatives that contribute to its growth.

11.1 The Bitcoin SV Community

The Bitcoin SV community consists of a diverse group of individuals, including developers, entrepreneurs, investors, and enthusiasts who share a common interest in advancing the capabilities and adoption of BSV. This community is characterized by its passion for the original vision of Bitcoin as outlined by Satoshi Nakamoto and its commitment to building on top of the Bitcoin SV blockchain.

11.2 Values and Principles

The Bitcoin SV community is driven by a set of core values and principles:

11.2.1 Scalability and Efficiency:

The community recognizes the importance of scalability to enable a high volume of transactions and support a growing user base. Scalability solutions and advancements in transaction throughput are seen as crucial for achieving widespread adoption.

11.2.2 Security and Stability: The community places a strong emphasis on the security and stability of the Bitcoin SV network. This includes maintaining a decentralized consensus mechanism, ensuring the immutability of the blockchain, and implementing robust security measures to protect user funds and data.

11.2.3 Original Vision of Bitcoin: The Bitcoin SV community is committed to preserving and advancing the original vision of Bitcoin as outlined by Satoshi Nakamoto. This includes promoting peer-to-peer electronic cash, enabling smart contracts and tokenization, and embracing the principles of decentralization and transparency.

11.2.4 Innovation and Development: The community fosters a culture of innovation and continuous development. This includes supporting research and development efforts, providing resources and tools for developers, and encouraging the creation of new applications, services, and technologies on the Bitcoin SV blockchain.

11.3 Achievements and Milestones

The Bitcoin SV community has achieved significant milestones since the creation of the network. Some notable achievements include:

11.3.1 Genesis Upgrade: The successful implementation of the Genesis upgrade, which restored the original Bitcoin protocol and set the stage for further development and innovation on the Bitcoin SV blockchain.

11.3.2 Scaling Progress: The ongoing advancements in scaling, including the increase in block size limits, to facilitate higher transaction throughput and address the scalability challenge.

11.3.3 Metanet Framework: The introduction of the Metanet framework, which combines blockchain and the internet to create a new paradigm for data storage, management, and monetization.

11.3.4 Developer Support: The growth of a vibrant developer community with a wide range of tools, libraries, and resources to support the development of applications and services on the Bitcoin SV blockchain.

11.4 The Ecosystem and Projects

The Bitcoin SV ecosystem is expanding rapidly, with a diverse range of projects and initiatives across various industries. Some notable projects include:

11.4.1 Tokenization Platforms: Platforms that enable the creation and management of tokens on the Bitcoin SV blockchain, facilitating asset tokenization and opening up new opportunities for investment and ownership.

11.4.2 Smart Contract Development: Development of smart contract platforms and frameworks that leverage the programmability of the Bitcoin SV blockchain to create decentralized applications and automated agreements.

11.4.3 Supply Chain Solutions: Projects focused on leveraging Bitcoin SV's transparency and traceability to revolutionize supply chain management, ensuring authenticity, reducing fraud, and enhancing trust.

11.4.4 Data Management and Monetization: Initiatives that explore the potential of Metanet for data storage, management, and monetization, enabling individuals to have greater control over their digital assets and data.

11.4.5 Education and Adoption: Efforts to educate individuals and businesses about Bitcoin SV, promote its adoption, and foster a broader understanding of blockchain technology and its potential.

The Bitcoin SV community and ecosystem are instrumental in the growth and development of the platform. With its shared values, achievements, and diverse range of projects, the community contributes to the scalability, security, and innovation of Bitcoin

SV. As the ecosystem continues to expand, collaboration and support within the community will be crucial for achieving the vision of a global, scalable blockchain platform that empowers individuals and transforms industries.

Chapter 12

Conclusion and Outlook for Bitcoin SV

Bitcoin SV (BSV) has emerged as a blockchain platform with a clear vision and a focus on scalability, security, and real-world utility. In this final chapter, we will recap the key highlights of Bitcoin SV, reflect on its journey so far, and explore the potential future outlook for this innovative blockchain platform.

12.1 Recap of Key Highlights

Throughout this book, we have explored various aspects of Bitcoin SV. We learned about its origins and the scaling debate within the Bitcoin community. We discussed the Genesis upgrade, which restored the original Bitcoin protocol and paved the way for technical advancements and innovations. We explored smart contracts, tokenization, and the

Metanet framework, which unlocked new possibilities for programmability, asset representation, and data management. We also delved into real-world use cases, the community, and the growing ecosystem surrounding Bitcoin SV.

12.2 Reflections on Bitcoin SV's Journey

Bitcoin SV has come a long way since its inception. It has made significant strides in addressing the scalability challenge, maintaining the security and integrity of the network, and advancing the capabilities of the blockchain. The community has played a vital role in driving development, fostering innovation, and promoting the original vision of Bitcoin. The ecosystem has witnessed the emergence of diverse projects and initiatives that leverage the unique features of Bitcoin SV, contributing to its growth and adoption.

12.3 Future Outlook for Bitcoin SV

The future of Bitcoin SV holds great potential and several challenges. Looking ahead, there are several key areas to watch:

12.3.1 Scalability and Adoption:

Bitcoin SV will continue to focus on scaling to accommodate increased adoption and transaction throughput. Efforts to simplify user experiences, enhance user interfaces, and drive merchant acceptance will contribute to its wider adoption.

12.3.2 Regulatory Compliance: Navigating evolving regulatory frameworks and striking a balance between compliance, privacy, and decentralization will be crucial for Bitcoin SV's growth and acceptance by institutions and mainstream users.

12.3.3 Interoperability and Integration: Collaborations and partnerships with other blockchain platforms and traditional systems will foster interoperability and integration. Standardization efforts and cross-platform compatibility will enable seamless data exchange and broader utility.

12.3.4 Continued Innovation: Ongoing research and

development will drive technical advancements, such as privacy solutions, smart contract functionality, and tokenization capabilities. The community's support for developers and the creation of developer-friendly tools and resources will foster further innovation.

12.4 The Power of Bitcoin SV

Bitcoin SV has demonstrated its potential to transform industries, drive innovation, and empower individuals. Its scalability, security, and programmability make it well-suited for a wide range of applications, from supply chain management to healthcare records, content publishing to gaming, and beyond. The vision of a decentralized, transparent, and scalable blockchain platform is within reach.

In conclusion, Bitcoin SV is poised to continue its journey of growth and development. With its strong community, expanding ecosystem, and a commitment to the original vision of Bitcoin, Bitcoin SV has the potential to reshape industries, create new economic opportunities, and bring about meaningful change in the digital landscape. As the world embraces the possibilities of blockchain technology, Bitcoin SV stands ready to be a leader in the next era of decentralized systems and digital interactions.

The End.